WASPS

by Sylvia A. Johnson

Photographs by Hiroshi Ogawa

A Lerner Natural Science Book

Lerner Publications Company ▪ Minneapolis

Sylvia A. Johnson, Series Editor

Translation of original text by Kay Kushino

Photograph on page 27 by Satoshi Kuribayashi

*The publisher wishes to thank Jerry W. Heaps,
Department of Entomology, University of Minnesota,
for his assistance in the preparation of this book.*

The glossary on page 46 gives definitions and pronunciations
of words shown in **bold type** in the text.

LIBRARY OF CONGRESS CATALOGING IN PUBLICATION DATA

Johnson, Sylvia A.
  Wasps.

  (A Lerner natural science book)
  Adaptation of: Ashinagabachi / by Hiroshi Ogawa.
  Includes index.
  Summary: A description of those wasps which are social insects,
discussing their nest building, egg laying, metamorphic develop-
ment, and life in their colony.
  1. Wasps—Juvenile literature. 2. Insect societies—Juvenile
literature. [1. Wasps. 2. Insect societies] I. Ogawa, Hiroshi.
Ashinagabachi. II. Title. III. Series.
QL565.2.J64 1984   595.79'8   83-23847
ISBN 0-8225-1460-5 (lib. bdg.)

International Standard Book Number: 0-8225-1460-5
Library of Congress Catalog Card Number: 83-23847

5   6   7   8   9   10   93

Many people are well acquainted with wasps. During the warm months of summer, the black-and-gold insects are often seen hovering near barns and houses or zooming down to land on food left out on picnic tables. Humans usually think of wasps as pests or fear them because of the unpleasant stings they can inflict. But very few know much about what kind of insects wasps are or how they spend their time when they are not bothering people.

This book describes the hidden lives of wasps and the amazing skills they use in making their nests, collecting food, and raising their young.

One good way to find out something about wasps is to discover who their relatives are in the insect world. Wasps are closely related to two other familiar groups of insects, bees and ants. All three groups belong to the scientific order Hymenoptera, and they have many characteristics in common.

The word **Hymenoptera,** which means "membrane wings," refers to the two pairs of stiff, transparent wings that are found on many members of the order. Another physical feature shared by most Hymenoptera insects is a slender "waist" in the middle part of the body that makes it unusually flexible. Most Hymenoptera also have a sting or some other poison-ejecting device located on the last section of their bodies.

One of the most unusual characteristics shared by many Hymenoptera is a communal way of life. All ants and many bees and wasps live together in communities where they share food and cooperate in raising young. This unique pattern of behavior has earned them the name **social insects**.

Not all wasps are social insects, but those that do live in groups are the ones seen most often by humans. Among the social wasps are the familiar insects called yellow jackets and hornets. They belong to the family Vespidae, along with another very common group of social wasps known by the scientific name *Polistes* (po-LIH-steez). Most of the wasps shown in this book are members of this group.

In order to find out how social wasps live, let's follow a *Polistes* wasp through the yearly cycle of its life.

The best time of year to begin observing *Polistes* wasps is spring. When the warm weather and longer days of spring arrive, a *Polistes* wasp like the one shown above emerges from its long winter hibernation, ready to continue its active life.

Left: A *Polistes* wasp laps up nectar from a dandelion. *Opposite:* A field full of spring flowers provides nourishing food for hungry wasps.

Polistes wasps spend the winter hibernating in small groups, hidden away in hollow logs and other protected places. The hibernating wasps have one important thing in common: they are all females that are capable of laying eggs. After emerging from hibernation, these wasps will have the responsibility of establishing new wasp colonies.

The very first thing that a wasp does after leaving hibernation is to look for food. The insect has spent several months without eating, and the food energy stored in her body is almost used up. Before tackling the big job ahead, the wasp must eat.

Like their cousins the bees, many kinds of adult wasps, including *Polistes,* eat flower nectar. They push their tongue-like mouthparts deep into flowers and lap up the sweet liquid.

Left and Opposite: A foundress wasp collects wood fiber for her nest.

After strengthening herself with food, a female wasp begins the work of establishing a new community. Sometimes several *Polistes* females will cooperate in this job, but frequently a single female will be the **foundress** of the colony.

Like all family groups, a wasp colony needs a place to live and the first job of the foundress is building a nest for her future family. The nests of social wasps are constructed out of paperlike material made from plant fibers. A foundress wasp collects fibers from dry grasses, old boards, fence posts, and many other sources. She pulls up pieces of these materials with her **mandibles,** or jaws, and chews them into a pulp, adding plenty of saliva. Then she carries the pulp in her mouth to the spot where she will build her nest.

A wasp brings a mouthful of wood pulp to the spot where she is building her nest.

Polistes wasps build their nests in all kinds of places. Sometimes they construct them out in the open, attaching them to plant stems and branches. Other *Polistes* nests are built in sheltered spots, in crevices or under the eaves of houses and garages.

Wherever a *Polistes* wasp constructs her nest, she usually starts the job by attaching a small dab of pulp to a horizontal surface. Adding more pulp, she extends the dab into a thin stem, or **pedicel,** which will eventually support the whole nest.

After she has finished the pedicel, the wasp brings more pulp to form the first individual **cell** of the nest. Using her mouthparts and legs, she shapes and smooths the pulp into a cone-shaped chamber attached to the end of the pedicel. As she works, she keeps the pulp moist by adding water from a supply stored in her body.

This *Polistes* wasp is constructing her nest on a barbed-wire fence. She first forms the pedicel, the stem from which the nest will hang (above left). Then she uses her mouthparts and legs to shape wood pulp into a cone-shaped cell (above right and right). In these pictures, you can see how a wasp's narrow "waist" makes it possible for the insect to bend and twist its body.

13

Left: The foundress lays her first egg. *Opposite:* This cross-section picture of a wasp nest shows several eggs inside their cells. The eggs are fastened to the cell walls by the eggs' sticky coverings.

As soon as the female *Polistes* has finished the first cell of her nest, she begins to carry out the other important part of her job as foundress of the new colony. She lays a single egg inside the cell.

Before she entered her winter hibernation, the female mated with one or more male wasps. The males' sperm, or reproductive cells, are now stored inside her body in a chamber called the **spermatheca.** As the female's egg is laid, it is united with a sperm cell released from the spermatheca. This **fertilized egg** will eventually develop into a young wasp, the first new member of the colony.

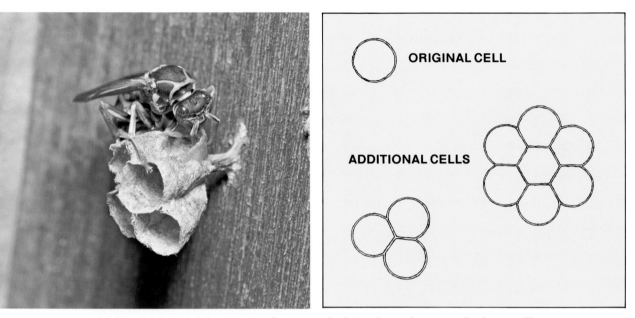

As a wasp nest grows larger (left), the shape of the cells begins to change (right).

ORIGINAL CELL

ADDITIONAL CELLS

After laying her first egg, the foundress wasp goes back to the task of making more cells for the nest. She forms each new cell right next to the ones already constructed so that it can share the same walls. The original cell in the nest was cone-shaped, but as other cells are built against it, its walls flatten out to form a six-sided chamber. As the nest grows, it develops into a cluster of six-sided cells suspended from the pedicel.

The size of the foundress's family grows just as fast as her nest does. As soon as the female finishes each new cell, she immediately lays an egg in it.

In *Polistes* nests established by more than one foundress, a slightly different kind of development may take place. The wasps share the job of constructing cells, but they cannot all be egg-layers. Like a beehive, a wasp nest can have only one **queen,** or female who has the primary responsibility of laying eggs.

In order to determine which foundress will be queen, *Polistes* wasps may have an egg-laying contest. Several females build cells and lay eggs in them as fast as they can. At the same time, they eat the eggs laid by their rivals and lay their own eggs in the empty cells.

Eventually the female with the best egg-laying ability (and the biggest appetite) is recognized as the winner of the contest. She is established as queen of the nest, and the other foundress wasps become her helpers.

When a wasp colony has more than one foundress, the size of the nest increases rapidly.

Opposite: A foundress wasp on her nest. *Right:* Wasp larvae inside their cells. Their dark heads can be seen at the openings of the cells.

When there is only one foundress in a nest, she must do all the work by herself. Building cells and laying eggs are big jobs, but when the eggs begin to hatch, the foundress really has no time to spare.

The eggs of most *Polistes* wasps hatch about two weeks after they are laid. What comes out of an egg is not a baby wasp but a wormlike creature without legs or wings. It is a wasp larva, the second of the four stages in the development that produces an adult wasp. This complicated process of development is called **metamorphosis.** Bees, ants, and many other kinds of insects also go through metamorphosis before they become adults.

In order to develop, a wasp larva needs nourishment, and a lot of it. Its mother, the foundress of the colony, must provide food for her offspring. Like an adult wasp, a larva eats some nectar, but the most important part of its diet is meat. To supply the larva with the meat it needs, the mother wasp assumes the job of **predator,** or hunter.

19

This female wasp has captured a butterfly caterpillar.

The **prey** that a *Polistes* female captures most often is another insect, particularly insect larvae like butterfly caterpillars and beetle grubs. She seizes small insects in her powerful mandibles and carries them back to the nest, where they will be torn in pieces to feed the wasp larvae. If the insect is a large one, she will chew off a piece of its flesh and take that to the nest. A *Polistes* hunter usually does not sting her prey unless it attacks her.

At the nest, the wasp prepares a piece of meat for the larvae by chewing it herself. Then she taps with her head on the rim of one of the cells to let a larva know that its meal is ready.

This signal causes the larva to poke its head out of the chamber, as shown in the picture on the opposite page. The female wasp pushes the chewed-up meat against the larva's face, and the larva pulls off a piece with its mouthparts. Then the female moves on to feed the occupant of another cell.

A larva being fed
by an adult wasp

The dragonfly captured by this wasp will provide food for hungry larvae.

The larvae shown in the cells on the right have almost completed their development. The covered cells on the left contain pupae, the next stage in a wasp's metamorphosis.

A *Polistes* larva spends about two weeks inside its cell, eating and growing. During this time, its size increases enormously, and the mother wasp must add more pulp to the rim of the cell to make room for her rapidly growing offspring.

During the period of larval development, a wasp larva **molts,** or sheds the outer covering of its body, several times. Like all insects' bodies, the larva's body is covered with material that does not stretch. In order for the larva to grow, the old covering must be discarded and replaced by a new, larger one that develops underneath it.

After the larva has molted about four times, it stops eating and prepares to enter a new stage of its metamorphosis. It is now ready to become a **pupa.**

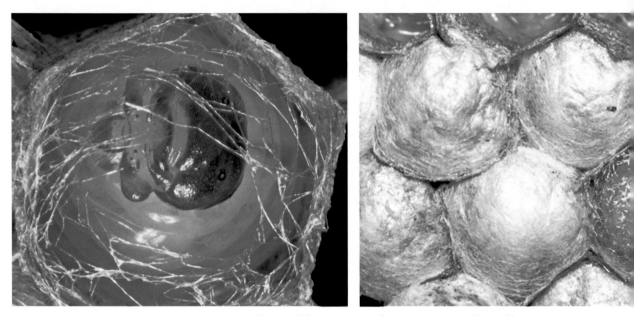

Left: A larva spinning the silken cap for its pupal cell. *Right:* When the cap is finished, it will completely seal the cell opening.

To prepare for this new stage, the larva begins to seal itself inside its cell. It sends out fine silk thread from an organ on its head called a **spinneret.** Moving its head back and forth, the larva spins a thick, silk cap or lid that seals the opening of the cell. It also lines the cell with a thin layer of silk.

Shut up inside its cell, the larva molts one final time. Underneath the old larval skin is an entirely different form of the developing wasp—the pupa.

The pupal stage of the wasp's metamorphosis is a time of great change. During this period, the wormlike, eyeless larva is transformed into an adult wasp with its large eyes,

24

long legs, and strong wings. This change takes place as the tissues of the larva's body are gradually broken down and reformed into the body parts of an adult wasp.

The pupal stage of a *Polistes* wasp lasts about three weeks. Since the mother wasp laid her eggs at different times, the wasp pupae in one nest complete their development at different times. But by the beginning of summer, the foundress is no longer the only adult wasp in the nest.

During the pupal stage, the wormlike larva (left) will gradually be transformed into an adult wasp (right).

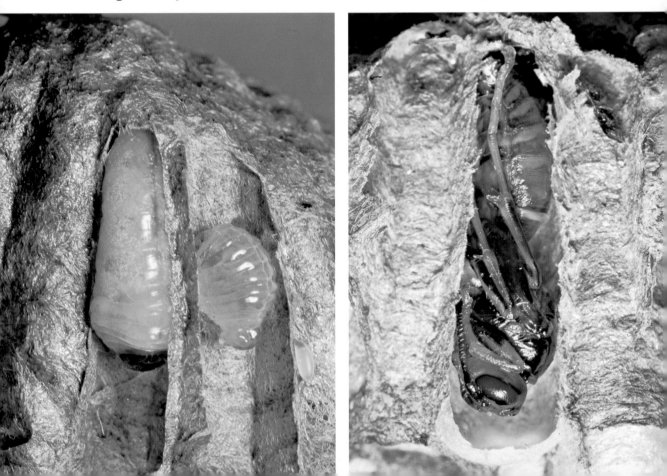

One by one, the sealed cells break open, and the new members of the wasp colony emerge. They are fully developed adult wasps, all descended from the same mother. The new young wasps have one more important thing in common: they are all females.

26

Like worker wasps, a worker in an ant colony (right) helps the queen (left) to care for the larvae and pupae.

These young females will have a very different role in the wasp community from that of their mother, the foundress and queen. They will be the workers of the colony, building cells, collecting food, and doing other jobs around the nest. Instead of laying eggs and producing young of their own, they will help the queen to take care of her offspring, their younger sisters.

The same division of labor between the queen and a large number of helpers also exists in colonies of ants and social bees. Only one other group of insects, the termites (order Isoptera), has this kind of complicated social system.

Left: A wasp nest covered with busy workers. *Right:* As *Polistes* workers add cells to a nest, it may take on a distorted shape.

After emerging from their cells, the worker wasps rest for a few days on the outside of the nest, cleaning themselves and exercising their wings. Then their instincts tell them that it is time to get to work.

One of the important jobs performed by the workers is adding new cells to the nest and repairing old ones. The young workers take over this task from the queen so that she can devote all her time to laying eggs. As more and more workers emerge and join the labor force, the nest rapidly gets bigger, with many new cells added to its outer edges. By the end of the summer, the nest has reached its largest size, containing perhaps as many as 250 cells.

A *Polistes* nest surrounded by green summer leaves. The summer season is the time of greatest activity in a wasp colony.

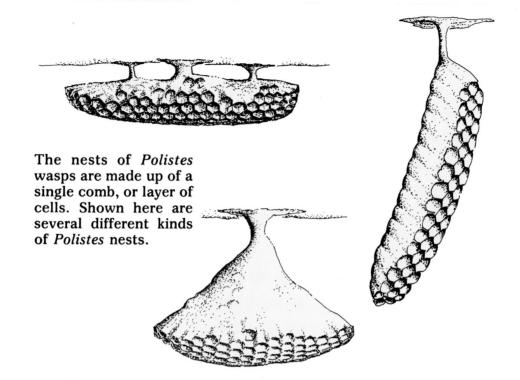

The nests of *Polistes* wasps are made up of a single comb, or layer of cells. Shown here are several different kinds of *Polistes* nests.

The nests of many other social wasps, including hornets and yellow jackets, consist of several combs suspended one under the other. The entire nest is enclosed in layers of paper.

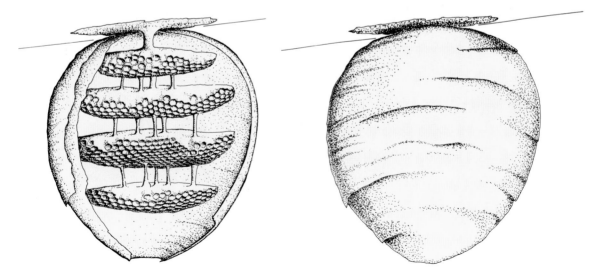

Before young *Polistes* workers first leave the nest to collect wood pulp for cell building, they make sure that they can find their way back home. They do this by taking an orientation flight around the nest, hovering near it and flying around it again and again. In these flights, the wasps seem to be using their eyesight to learn the location of the nest and landmarks around it. On longer journeys, wasps probably find their way home by remembering the position of the sun in relation to their line of flight.

Workers leave the nest to collect not only pulp but also food. They take over the queen's job of capturing insects, chewing them up, and feeding them to the hungry larvae. With so many workers to feed them, the larvae that hatch in mid-summer get more food than the earlier larvae that were fed by the queen alone. These larvae usually develop into adult wasps that are bigger and stronger than the first workers.

Adult wasps sharing food as they hang upside down on the nest

When a worker wasp comes back to the nest with part of an insect, she often shares the food with the other adult wasps. Several wasps gather around the returning worker and bite off a piece of the meat she is carrying. After chewing up their share of the food, they eat some of it themselves and distribute the rest to the larvae.

33

Left: A *Polistes* wasp collects water to be used in cooling the nest. *Opposite:* Wing fanning also helps to reduce the temperature inside the wasp nest.

The *Polistes* workers also have the job of controlling the temperature of the nest. During the hot days of summer, the interior of the wasp nest may become too warm for the developing larvae and pupae. In order to prevent this, the workers set up a natural system of air conditioning.

The wasp brings water to the nest in her **crop,** a second stomach used to store food or water. She scatters the water on the outside walls and inside empty cells. The evaporation of the water lowers the temperature inside the nest.

The workers sometimes add to the effectiveness of the cooling system by sitting on the outside of the nest and fanning their wings. The resulting breeze increases the rate of evaporation and helps to produce an ideal climate for the development of the young inside the nest.

These two pictures show the queen of a hornet colony making a raid on a *Polistes* nest. On the opposite page, you can see the queen attacking a pupa she has pulled from its cell. Hornets (genus *Vespa*) are bigger than their *Polistes* relatives, and hornet queens are particularly large and powerful.

In addition to all their other tasks, worker wasps may be called upon to defend their nest against attack by enemies. All the workers and the queen are equipped with stings at the ends of their abdomens that can be used to inject poison into an attacker. *Polistes* workers are not easily aroused, but they will try to sting animals, including humans, that disturb their nests. A worker bee usually dies after stinging because its sting sticks in the body of the attacker, pulling away part of the bee's own body. A wasp sting, however, can be pulled out and used again and again.

Many of the enemies that threaten a *Polistes* nest are other insects, particularly other kinds of wasps. Some hornets, like the one shown on the opposite page, attack a nest and carry away the larvae and pupae, which they use to feed the young in their own nests.

Certain solitary wasps—those that do not live in communities—try to get into a *Polistes* nest so that they can

lay their own eggs in cells containing pupae. When the larvae hatch from the eggs, they eat the *Polistes* pupae and then go through their own development inside the borrowed pupal cells.

During most of the summer, the worker wasps keep busy at their jobs around the nest. The work force expands constantly as new workers complete their development and emerge from their cells. But as the summer days grow shorter, the population of the nest begins to change. The adult wasps that emerge from the cells in late summer do not join the workers in bringing food and repairing cells. Instead they remain idle, sitting on the outside of the nest.

The adults emerging in late summer are not workers at all but **reproductive** wasps. Their job is to make sure that a new generation of wasps will be born during the following year.

Some of the reproductive wasps are females, sisters of the workers and daughters of the queen and the male wasps that mated with her many months ago. Other reproductives are males. They are the brothers of the workers and sons of the queen, but unlike the workers and the reproductive females, they have no fathers.

Male wasps, like male bees and ants, develop only from unfertilized eggs. Hymenoptera queens have male sperm cells stored in their bodies, but they are capable of laying eggs that have not been fertilized by the sperm. These are the eggs that will develop into male insects. In some groups of Hymenoptera, including *Polistes* wasps, males can also develop from eggs laid by workers, females that have never mated.

Reproductive wasps on the outside of a nest

Left: The yellow faces of *Polistes* males set them apart from the females in the colony. *Opposite:* A *Polistes* nest in late summer. Some cells are still occupied by pupae, while many others are empty.

As more and more reproductive males and females appear in a *Polistes* nest, the life of the wasp community takes on a new pattern. The queen stops laying eggs, and the number of larvae needing food becomes increasingly smaller. Now the food brought back by the workers is fought over by the reproductives perched on the nest.

The reproductive wasps spend most of their time eating and grooming themselves, but they sometimes assist the workers by fanning their wings to help cool the nest.

By late summer, there is little activity in the *Polistes* nest. Having fulfilled her purpose in life, the queen of the colony is dead, and the other adult wasps have begun to leave the nest for long periods of time. The males are often chased away by the workers, who bite at them vigorously. They gather in small groups near the nest, waiting until the time comes when they can perform the job assigned to them in the life of the wasp community.

A pair of wasps mating. The male is on top of the female.

The job of the males is to mate with the reproductive females, who will be the foundresses of next year's wasp colonies. Mating takes place after all the adult wasps have left the nest. The males pursue the females, diving at them and seizing them with their legs. In mating, the bodies of a male and female wasp are joined, and sperm cells pass into the female's abdomen, where they are stored in the spermatheca.

After mating, most of the male wasps die, victims of predators or old age. The workers do not live long after leaving the nest either. Only the reproductive females survive the break-up of the wasp community.

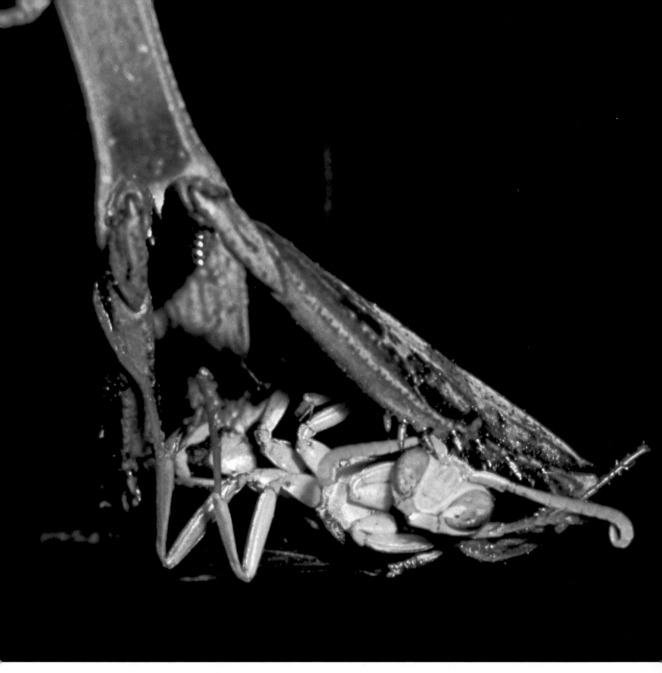

This male *Polistes* is being held by the powerful front legs
of a praying mantis. Because male wasps have no stings,
they cannot protect themselves against such predators.

Left: An abandoned wasp nest hanging from the leafless branch of a tree. *Opposite:* A group of *Polistes* females hibernating in a tree trunk.

After the wasps have gone, the nest hangs empty from its pedicel. Unlike a beehive or ant nest, it is used for only one season and then abandoned. The autumn rains and the snows of winter will begin to dissolve the paper cells so carefully constructed in the spring. The nest has served its purpose and is no longer needed.

After mating, the reproductive females, the surviving members of the *Polistes* community, find shelter in protected places. Huddled in small groups, they spend the winter in a state of hibernation. All their body functions slow down and their temperatures fall as low as 0 degrees Fahrenheit (−18 degrees Celsius).

In this state of inactivity, the female wasps live safely through the winter. When the warmth of spring rouses them, they leave their hiding places and begin to build the nests that will be home to a new generation of wasps.

44

GLOSSARY

cell—one of the individual chambers in a wasp nest

crop—a second stomach used to store water or food

fertilized egg—an egg that has been united with a male sperm cell

foundress—a female wasp that establishes a colony

Hymenoptera (hi-meh-NOP-teh-ruh)—the scientific order to which wasps belong. Bees and ants are also members of this order.

larva—the second stage in complete metamorphosis, during which the insect is usually legless and wormlike. The plural form of the word is larvae, pronounced LAR-vee.

mandibles (MAN-di-buhls)—insect jaws used to hold and chew food. Wasps also use their mandibles in building their nests.

metamorphosis (met-uh-MOR-fuh-sis)—the process of growth and change that produces most adult insects. Wasps, bees, ants, and many other kinds of insects go through a four-stage development known as complete metamorphosis; the four stages are egg, larva, pupa, and adult. Another process of development called incomplete metamorphosis has only three stages: egg, nymph, and adult.

molt—to shed the outer covering of the body

pedicel (PED-ih-sel)—the stem from which a wasp nest hangs

predator—an animal that hunts and kills other animals for food

prey—an animal killed by another animal and used for food

queen—the primary egg-laying female in a colony of social insects

pupa (PEW-puh)—the third stage in complete metamorphosis, during which the larva is transformed into an adult insect. The plural form of the word is **pupae,** pronounced PEW-pee.

reproductive wasp—a wasp able to mate and produce young

social insects—insects that live groups, sharing food and cooperating in raising young

spinneret (spin-uh-RET)—an organ on an insect's head through which silk thread is expelled

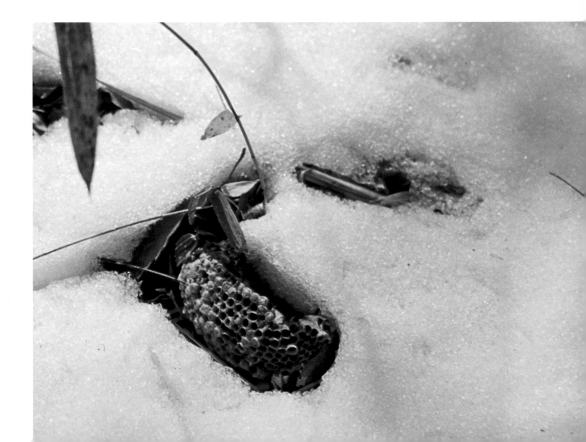

INDEX